This Journal Belongs To

....

Made in the USA
Monee, IL
28 May 2026